0301542

MORRIS AUTOMATED INFORMATION NETWORK

0 1021 0158469 0

ON LINE

Pull the other one!

STRING GAMES AND STORIES
BOOK 1

D0770035

Michael Taylor

Published by Hawthorn Press, Copyright © 2000

Hawthorn House, 1 Lansdown Lane, Stroud, Gloucestershire,

GL5 1BJ. Gt Britain

Tel. (01453) 757040 Fax. (01453) 751138

E-mail: hawthornpress@hawthornpress.com

Typeset at Hawthorn Press by Frances Fineran

Cover design by Patrick Roe at Southgate Solutions

Printed by The Cromwell Press, Trowbridge, Wiltshire

A catalogue record of this book is available from the British Library Cataloguing in Publication Data

ISBN 1 869 890 49 3

CONTENTS

CONTENTS

FOREWORD

The past decades have seen a significant erosion of childhood and a dwindling of childhood games and amusements. This has been noticed by many, bemoaned by some and actively challenged by a few. Michael Taylor is one of these few, for he has endeavoured to rescue an all-but-forgotten pastime that has delighted and intrigued children for centuries.

This book of string games, which is intended to be the first of a series, includes the much-loved Cat's Cradle and a selection of other patterns and tricks ranging from the very simple to the more complex. Anyone who can tie a shoelace will quickly grow to love these peaceful little string rituals. A child's coordination skills are strengthened by the intricate and rhythmic activity, and one can be assured that this will bring improvement both in concentration and mental dexterity.

How can one piece of string become so many different things, so quickly? String games are magic! See how the children, alive and busy in their imagination, gaze spellbound as the next form develops... Watch these same children magically grow in self-esteem as they learn to conjure the patterns themselves, and see how a new social dynamic is charmed into being as children begin to share and teach their new-found skills.

For several years Michael Taylor has helped us on the annual Lifeways Family Conference and Emerson

College in Sussex, England. He has entertained large groups of children with his stories and tricks, and triggered an epidemic of string games in all corners of the campus. We have seen how sharing pieces of string brings different age groups together and happily dissolves the language barriers between children of different nations.

String games are still nurtured in some far-flung communities of the world and given a place alongside folk tales and tribal histories as a precious and worthy education for real life. This book, and its future companion volumes, will be a valuable resource for any parent or teacher who wishes to offer children an artistic and healthy balance to our modern technological life.

Ann Druitt
Forest Row
23.10.99

STRING GAMES FROM AROUND THE WORLD

A friend of mine, who knows a few string games, recently went to Papua New Guinea... with a string in her pocket. (Did you know that was one of the definitions of an anthropologist at the turn of the century!)

In one village they didn't know any string games but they eagerly learnt a few. Yet in another village, not so far away, they showed her some very complicated figures.

In one a partner had to grab a fish before it disappeared. In another a bird actually made singing noises... when the string was plucked by the teeth!

Everyone enjoys a string story, especially when they can learn some games afterwards. And with practice everyone can learn... from about five years upwards.

A NOTE ABOUT THE DRAWINGS

Strings have sometimes been drawn shorter and thicker than they really are and hands more face-on than they would normally be in order to show relative positions more clearly.

Drawing strings going under and over each other is very much like drawing Celtic Knots... an ancient art in itself. Traditional artists have long found the process and results quite satisfying and readers might want to try it out on their own figures. Of course, if you want to also draw the hands... especially the writing hand... that is another problem!

How To Use This Book

1. As a Story Book

This book can be read as an illustrated story book – just read the large-typed pages and use a little imagination with the illustrations.

2. As an Instructional Manual for learning string games

Just pull out the string and follow the instructions. Remember, however, that Cat's Cradle is for two people. It is possible to make the Cat's Cradle sequence on your own, as the Japanese sometimes do, but they follow different instructions.

3. For telling stories while making string games

Although it is great fun just making the figures it is more entertaining if you say a few words at the same time. When the Eskimos play string games they often sing songs describing what the figure illustrates. In Murray Island, just north of Australia, string figure songs are called *Kamut Wed,* 'Kamut Songs'.

4. As a Springboard for the Imagination

As soon as you know a few string games you can try out some variations and invent your own stories and figures. If you make up some good ones send them to me, Michael Taylor, 9 Kidbrooke Rise, Forest Row, East Sussex, RH18 5LA, UK. If your figure or story is chosen for inclusion in a future book you'll get your name in print… and a free copy in the post!

AN INTRODUCTION TO STRING GAMES

EXAMPLES OF STRING FIGURES

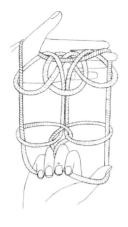

THE SUNFLOWER
An original continuation of
'The Well' – common in the
South Pacific Islands.

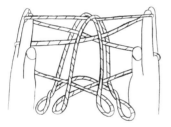

THE BELL
An original continuation of
'The Butterfly' – from Japan.

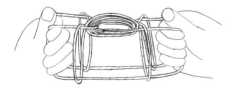

THE LITTLE PIG
This figure has been found in
South America.

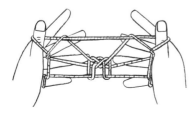

THE SEAGULL
An Eskimo string game.

Many shapes and patterns known as figures can be made from a loop of string held between the hands.

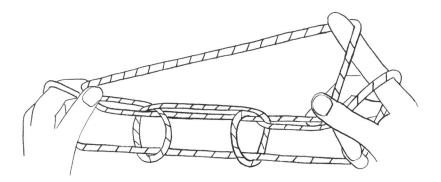

THE RACING CAR. An original continuation of the Navaho figure 'The Bird's Nest'.

NAMES AND STORIES

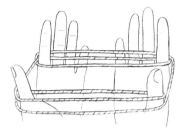

Candles (UK)
Chopsticks (Korea)
Mirror (Denmark)
River (Japan)

Soldier's Bed (UK)
Chessboard (Korea)
Church Window (UK)
Fishpond (America)

Cat's Eye (UK)
Cow's Eye (Korea)
Horse's Eye (Japan)

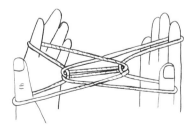

Fish on the Dish (UK)
Pig on the Pegs (UK)
A Musical Instrument
(Japan)

Each figure has a name.

Some have many names.

Sometimes songs are sung

and stories told while the

figures are being made.

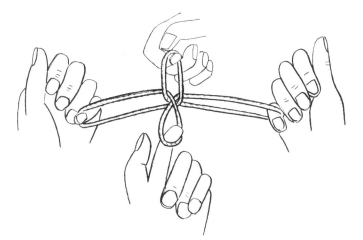

SAWING.
In Scotland they sing 'See-saw Johnnie Maw' while 'sawing'.
In India the Saw is called the Scissors.

STRING GAME TERMINOLOGY

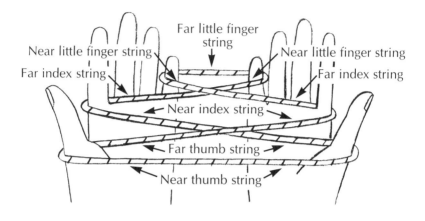

In the next picture you can find a near thumb string, a palm string, a near index string, a far index string, a near little finger string and upper and lower far little finger strings.

Can you see which is which?

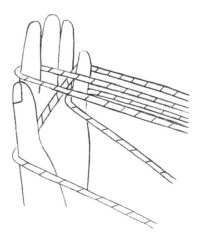

At the turn of the last century a terminology was developed to help record and teach string games.

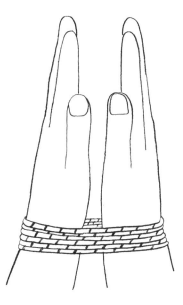

The 'Moat' has six wrist strings.

SPOT THE DIFFERENCE!

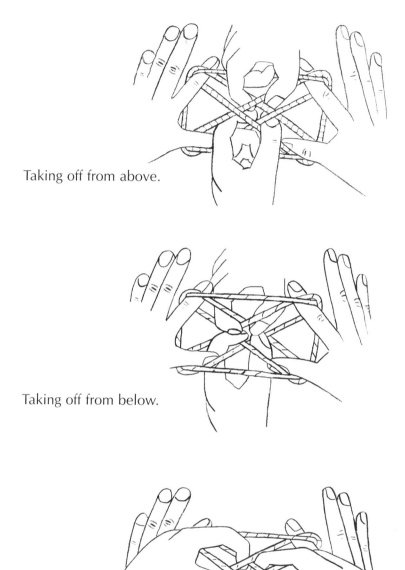

Taking off from above.

Taking off from below.

Taking off the wrong way!

Cat's Cradle is a game for two. It is also known as the 'Taking-Off Game' because one player has to take the strings from the other.

Two children playing Cat's Cradle

CAT'S CRADLE FOR TWO

THE CRADLE

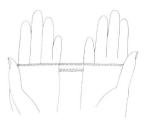

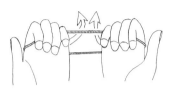

1. Place string circle around palms.

2. Close fingers over near string.

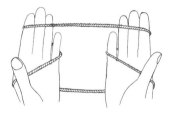

3. Turn fists away and open fingers between near and far lines.

4. Right middle finger takes left palm string from below.

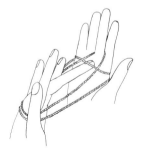

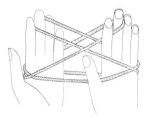

5. Repeat on other hand but stay between middle finger strings.

Once there was a man and a woman. They had a baby whom they rocked in a CRADLE.

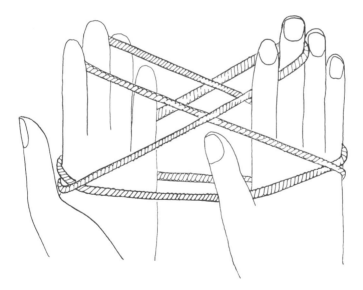

THE CRADLE

CRADLE TO SOLDIER'S BED

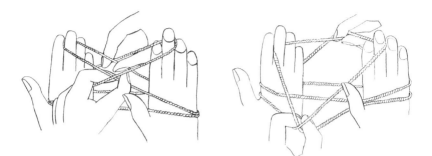

Pull pinched crosses over and back under framing strings.

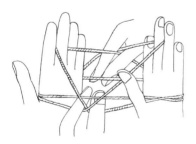

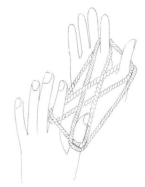

Lift off and open

They also had an older son.

He was a soldier and slept

on a SOLDIER'S BED.

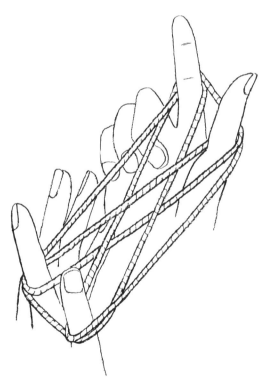

SOLDIER'S BED

SOLDIER'S BED TO CANDLES

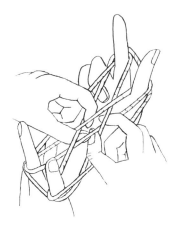

Pull pinched crosses over and back under framing strings.

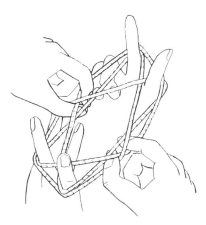

Lift off and open to reveal a box with two candles.

One day when the Mother was making CANDLES they heard a sound coming from the barn next door.

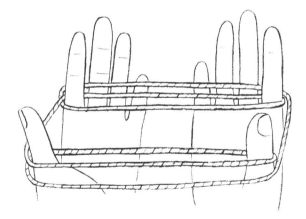

CANDLES

CANDLES TO MANGER

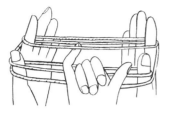

Hook far 'candle' string with upturned little finger, and pull.

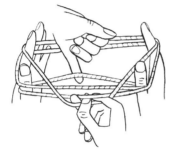

Repeat with other hand.

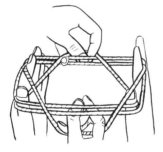

Pinch under framing strings.

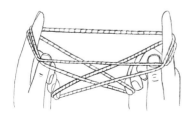

4. Lift off and open.

They went to investigate
and saw something
gleaming in the MANGER.

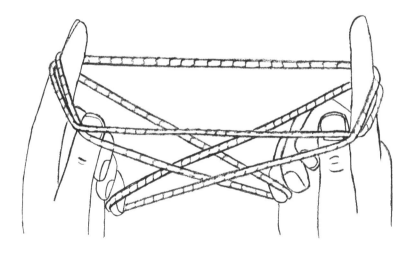

MANGER

MANGER TO DIAMONDS

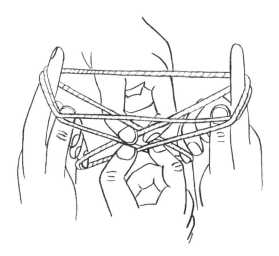

Pull pinched crosses over and down between framing strings.

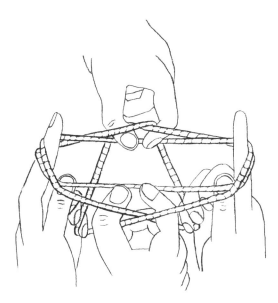

Pointing downwards, open and take off. See opposite page for finished figure.

Moving the straw aside

they found some glittering

DIAMONDS.

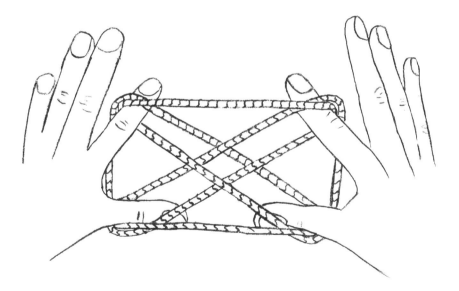

DIAMONDS

DIAMONDS TO CAT'S EYE

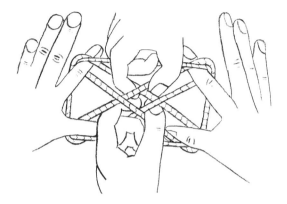

Pull pinched crosses over and back under framing strings.

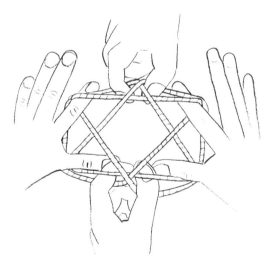

Lift off and open. See opposite page for finished figure.

Then they saw something else. A huge CAT'S EYE! The cat was watching and ready to pounce!

CAT'S EYE

CAT'S EYE TO FISH ON THE DISH

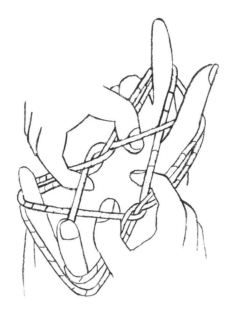

Pinch sides of 'eye'.

Turn upwards and lift off. See opposite for finished figure.

Thinking quickly, Mother went into the kitchen and returned with a tasty FISH ON THE DISH.

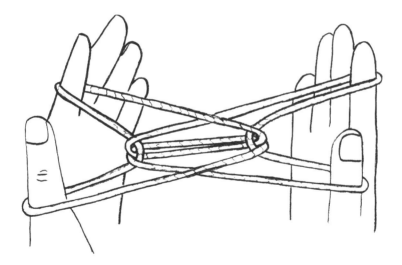

FISH ON THE DISH

FISH ON THE DISH TO HAND DRUM

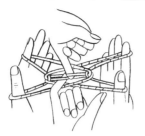

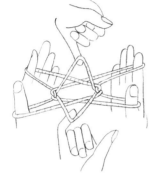

Hook near fish string with upturned little finger and pull.

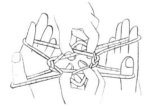

Repeat with other hand.

Pinch crosses of framing strings.

Turn upwards and lift off.

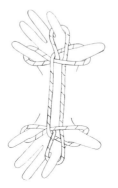

If 'Grandfather Clock' is formed instead of 'Hand Drum' (opposite page), the inner parallel strings have somehow become uncrossed and the game ends.

Suddenly they heard the
sound of a HAND DRUM.
Their son had returned!

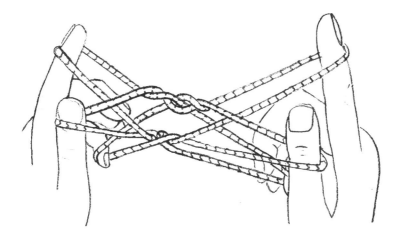

HAND DRUM

HAND DRUM TO DIAMONDS

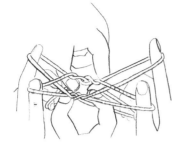

Pinch Hand Drum feet and pull.

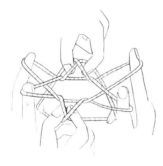

Turn up and over framing strings.

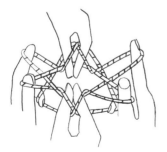

Pointing downwards, open and take off.

After kissing and hugging
him they showed him their
DIAMONDS...

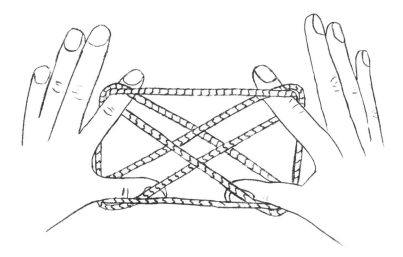

DIAMONDS

DIAMONDS TO CAT'S EYE (AGAIN)

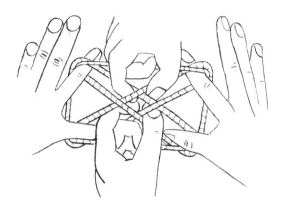

Pull pinched crosses over and back under framing strings.

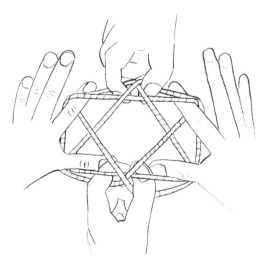

Lift off and open.

And their new cat, still purring, licking its lips and blinking its huge CAT'S EYE.

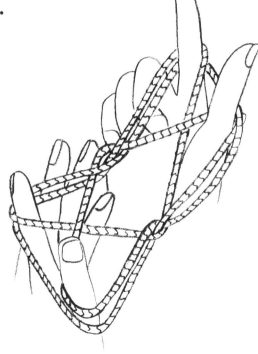

CAT'S EYE

CAT'S EYE TO MANGER

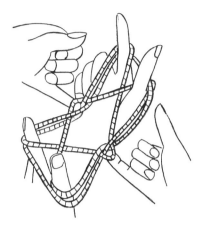

Hook curve of 'eye' in frame with upturned little fingers and pull.

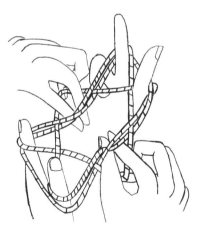

Pinch under framing strings.
Lift off and open.

They showed him the MANGER where they had found the diamonds.

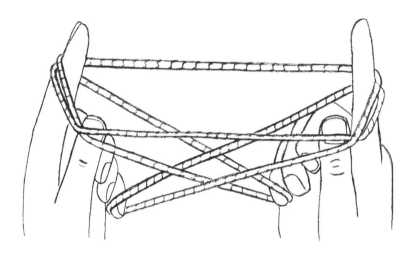

MANGER

MANGER TO SAWING

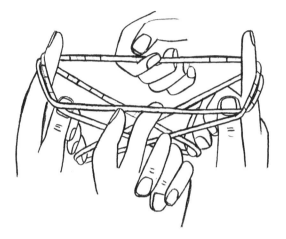

Take framing strings with indices.
Other player keeps little fingers.

Then Father and son began
SAWING firewood. That
night they sat by the fire…
But where was the cat?

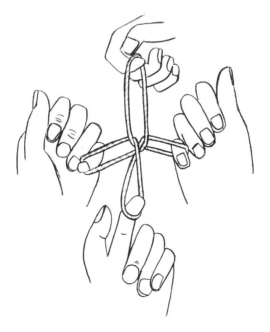

SAWING

ANOTHER WAY TO SAW

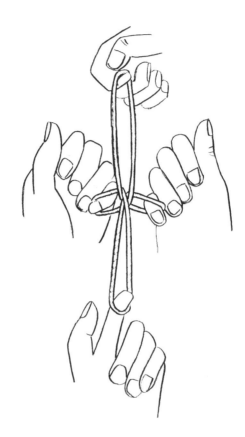

See what happens when your right hand swaps strings with your partner's left!

It had jumped into the cradle. So now you know why this story is called CAT'S CRADLE!

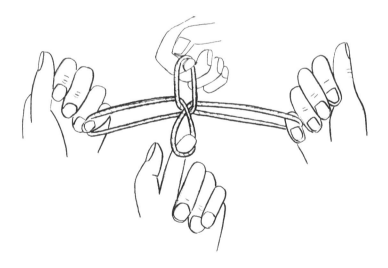

THE BIRTHDAY PARTY

BALLOONS

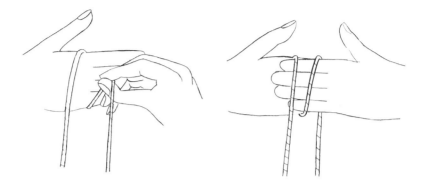

DOUBLE THE STRING by winding a single strand twice around your palm and lifting it.

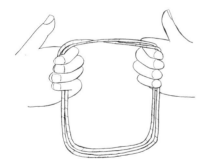

You now have a doubled loop.

To throw balloons high into the air... turn, lift and let go!

Once there was a Birthday Party. First, balloons were made.

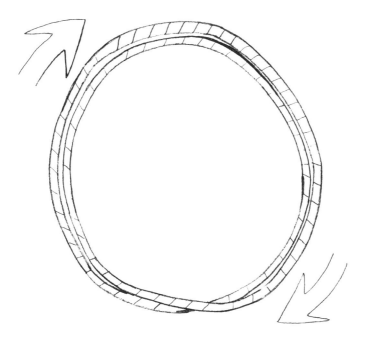

A BALLOON

THE TABLE-CLOTH

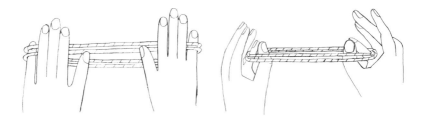

Hold doubled loop on little fingers. Thumbs, pointing the same way, join them.

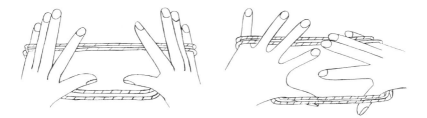

Little fingers hardly move as thumbs move down and away from them catching far strings on their backs.

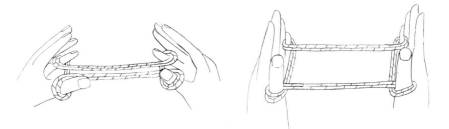

Hands assuming roof shape straighten up. Hands move together and apart to shake table-cloth (opposite page).

Then the table-cloth was
shaken.

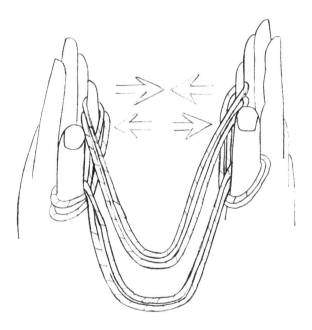

SHAKING THE TABLE-CLOTH

THE TABLE-CLOTH TO THE TABLE

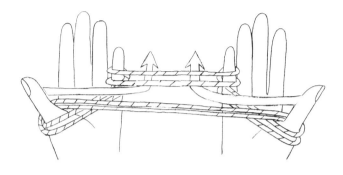

(1)

Thumbs take little finger strings from below (1) to make table (2) as seen by the audience (opposite page).

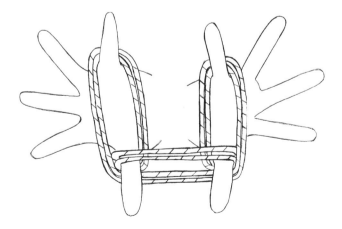

(2)

...and placed on the table.

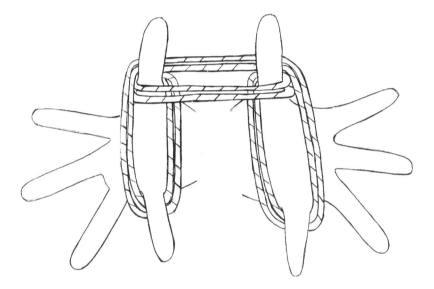

THE TABLE

THE TABLE TO THE CAKE

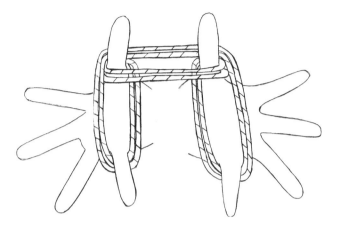

Hold little fingers together to make 'cake'.

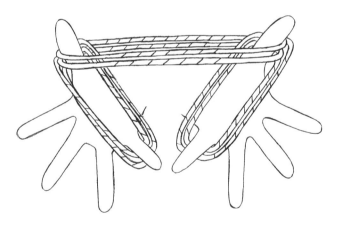

The cake was brought in.

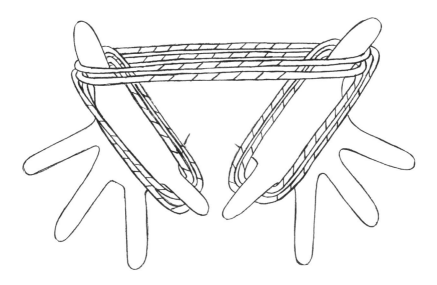

THE CAKE

THE CAKE TO THE LIT CANDLE TO THE EXTINGUISHED CANDLE

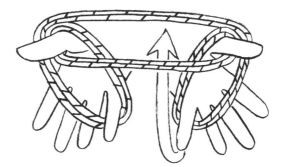

Little fingers take far thumb strings from below (those nearest to the little fingers!)

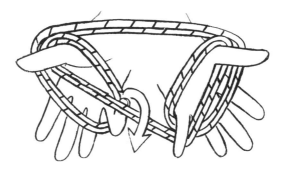

Light and extinguish candle by temporarily putting two outer palm strings between the fingers (opposite page).

and the candles were lit and

blown out.

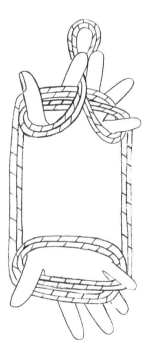

LIT CANDLE

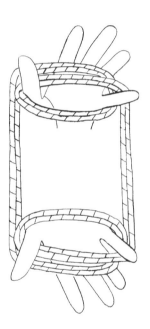

EXTINGUISHED CANDLE

THE EXTINGUISHED CANDLE TO THE ACCORDION

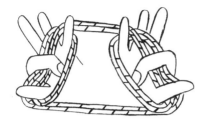

Index fingers dive down into the spaces between inner and outer palm strings

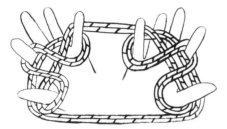

and stand up.

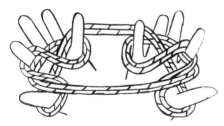

Long straight strings slip off thumbs

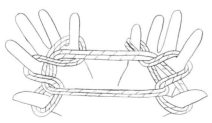

and little fingers.

Fingers splay apart and together, apart and together, to play accordion (opposite page). Don't forget too, to tap your right foot to keep time!

Pieces of cake were given
out and the music began.

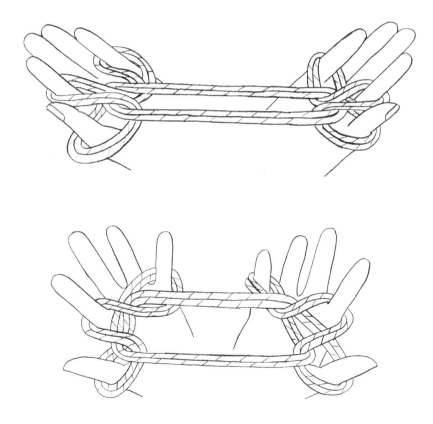

AN ACCORDION

THE ACCORDION TO THE SIX-POINTED STAR

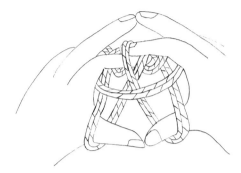

To make 'star' swap index loops. One loop goes through the other.

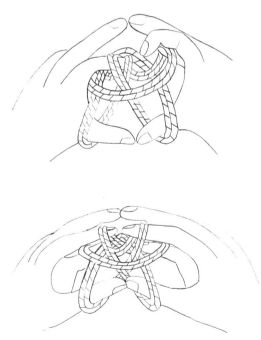

Games went on until the

stars came out.

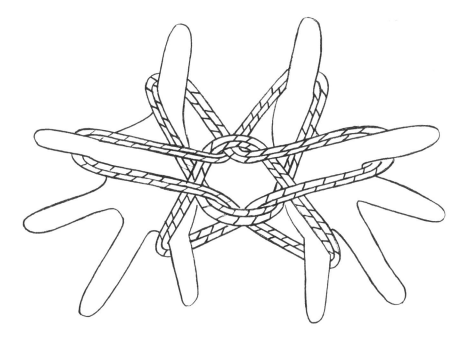

STAR

THE SIX-POINTED STAR TO THE GIFT

Release little fingers. Thumbs enter index loops from below.

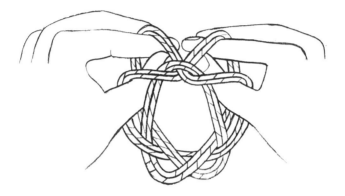

Remove index fingers from the loops, but do not pull hands apart. Little fingers followed by ring, middle and index enter thumb loops from the far side. Release thumbs.

Finally a party gift was given out.

GIFT

THE GIFT TO THE SUNGLASSES

(1)

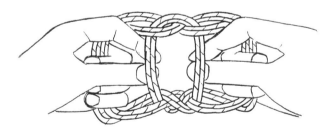

(2)

Thumbs (1) or thumbs and index fingers (2) catch sides of gift on their backs releasing other fingers. Pull apart.

In mine I found sunglasses.

When they broke I made

them again because…

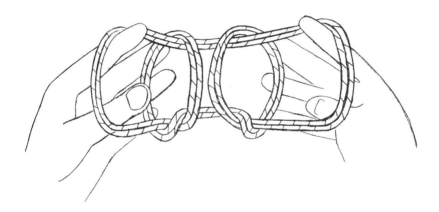

SUNGLASSES

WHEN THEY BREAK, MAKE THEM AGAIN!

Repeat the sequence noting:

If the gift does not form, you probably made the table (page 56) with the little fingers.

The gift opens well if laid down completely first but not if laid down back to front!

Sunglasses can be put back in their gift-box by first sliding (not folding) the lenses on top of each other to make a super-thick monocle and then by pulling the sides of the monocle out-wards (from behind or from in front), releasing all other strings at the same time.

…they were only made of string and in the party I had learnt how to make them!

Five-Pointed Star

LOOKING OUT OF THE WINDOW

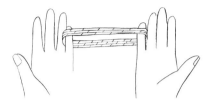

TREBLE THE LOOP by winding a strand three times around a palm and lifting the three palm strings.
Place the trebled loop on the little fingers.

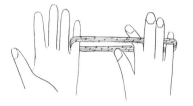

Little fingers hardly move as right index enters loop in the same direction,

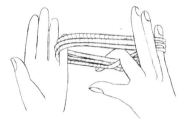

then points downwards,

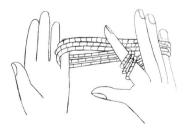

then points at left hand

and then up (opposite page).

Once a man looked out of a window. He looked down and then up at his friend.

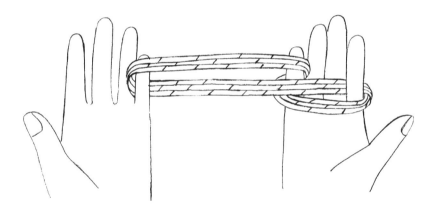

WINDOW TO CUP OF TEA TO TUNA SANDWICH

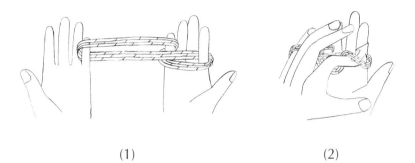

(1)   (2)

Left index shares right index loop from below (1 & 2) to make Cup of Tea. Teeth take near index strings temporarily to show Tuna Sandwich in the shape of a fish! (opposite page)

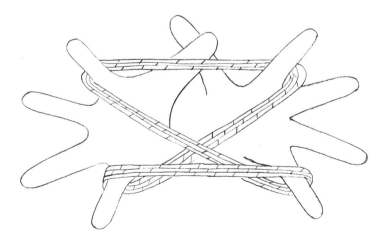

CUP OF TEA

His friend joined him for a cup of tea and a tuna sandwich.

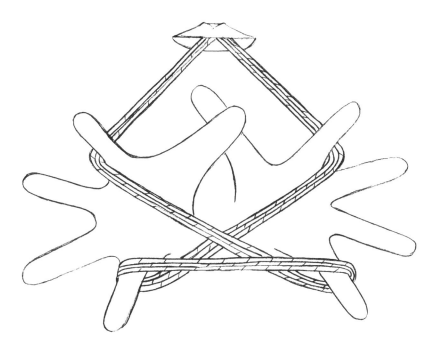

TUNA SANDWICH

TUNA SANDWICH TO CUP OF TEA TO FIVE-POINTED STAR

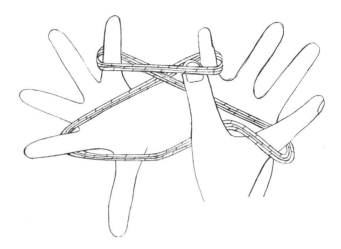

Right thumb bends over index strings to pick up straight near little finger 'saucer' string from below to make the five-pointed star (opposite page).

The stars come out.

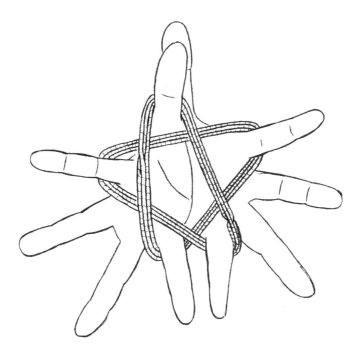

FIVE-POINTED STAR

FIVE-POINTED STAR TO MAN TO WINE GLASS TO CHAMPAGNE GLASS

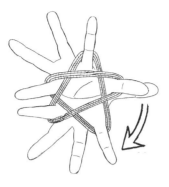

Hold left hand horizontally like a plate on a table.

Turn left hand clockwise like a record on a turntable to make the Man.

Drop his head to make a Wine Glass which turns into a Champagne Glass as hands pull apart. Untwist left hand (opposite page).

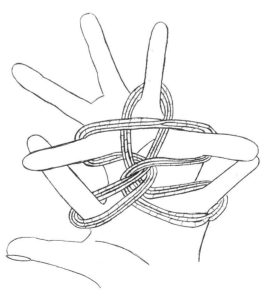

MAN

The man said 'Let's drink some wine and champagne!' So they did.

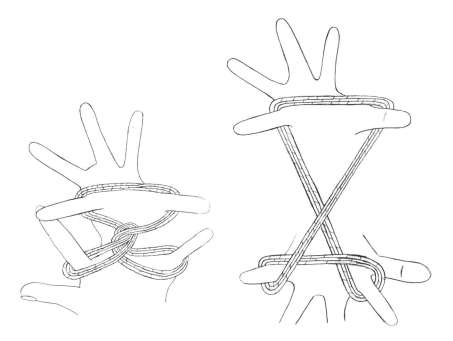

The WINE GLASS and the CHAMPAGNE GLASS
are made from the Man

A Sharp Knife

OPENING 'A'

First you need to DOUBLE THE STRING. See page 52.

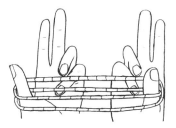

Place doubled loop on thumbs

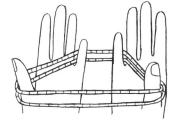

Little fingers enter loop from below.

Right index takes left palm strings.

Left index takes right palm strings.

If you ever have a very sharp

knife…

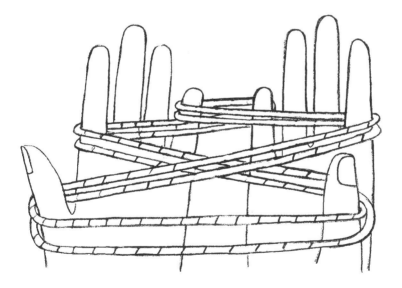

This is called OPENING 'A'

OPENING 'A' TO SHARP KNIFE

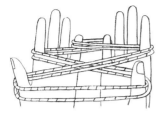

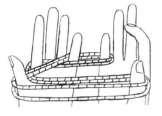

Drop right index.

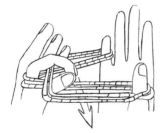

Left index hooks over palm string.

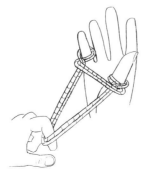

Release all left strings except hooked string.

…never ever touch the sharp end.

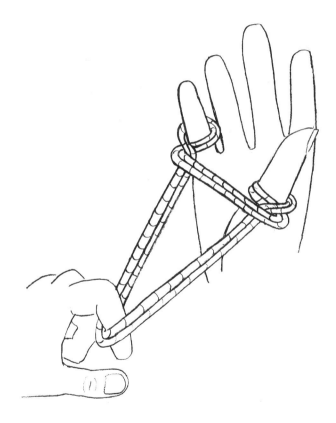

THE KNIFE

SHARP KNIFE TO BANDAGE

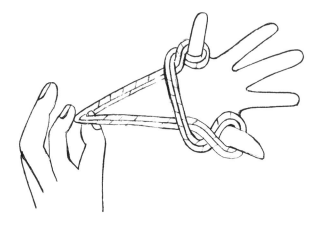

Transfer inside of knife point to left thumb and tap point with left index.

Remove right hand and wrap string several times around left index. Pull bandage off to reveal finger miraculously healed.

I did, and look what

happened!

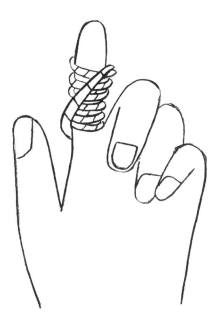

BANDAGE

ONE DAY IN PARIS

OPENING 'A' TO TWO FAT GENTLEMEN

Make Opening 'A' with single loop (see page 84).

Index fingers are 'ladies'.

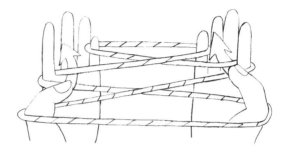

Thumbs ('gentlemen') bend over near index to pick up far index strings

Once a slim lady and another slim lady sat down with two fat gentlemen.

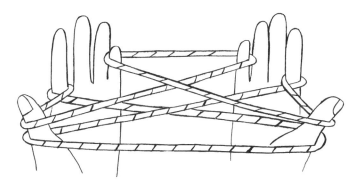

TWO FAT GENTLEMEN

TWO FAT GENTLEMEN TO CUP AND SAUCER

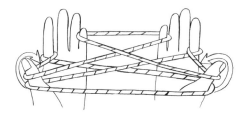

NAVAHO THE THUMB LOOPS! (When one finger or thumb has two loops and the lower loop is taken off over the upper loop it is called to 'navaho the loop'. This is because the Navaho People of North America use this method so often in their string figures.)

Drop the strings into the middle of the figure.

In the picture below the right hand is taking off the lower thumb loop. It can be done with the teeth.

Release little finger strings for 'Cup and Saucer'.

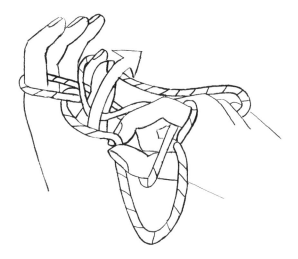

...for a cup of coffee.

While they were drinking,

a woman...

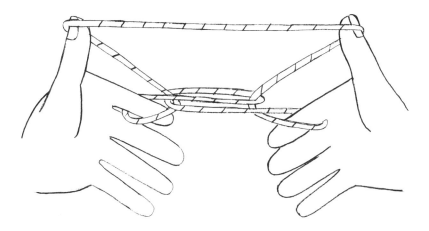

CUP AND SAUCER

CUP AND SAUCER TO WITCH'S HAT TO EIFFEL TOWER

Mouth takes thumb string.

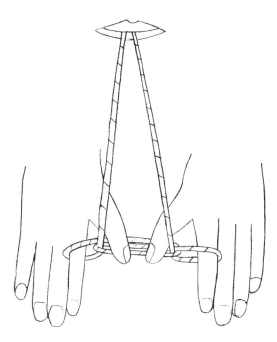

WITCH'S HAT

Hands turn, palm downwards, thumbs close together, little fingers far apart. 'Witch's Hat'.

Drop thumbs for 'Eiffel Tower'.

…with a witch's hat walked past. They followed her up the Eiffel Tower.

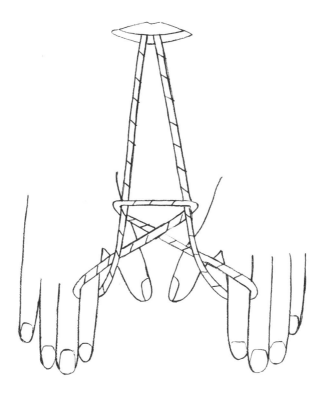

EIFFEL TOWER

EIFFEL TOWER TO SCARF

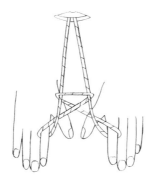

Hands pull apart to make 'coat-hanger' shape.

Drop mouth strings for 'scarf'.

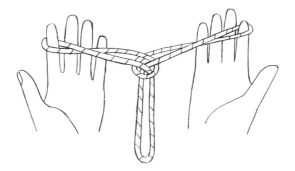

SCARF

Pull apart to make 'scarf' disappear.

When they got to the top

only her scarf remained.

Then even that disappeared.

She must have been a witch!

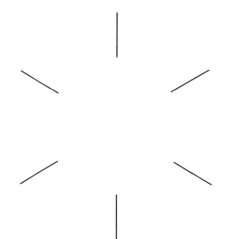

FIGURES INVENTED BY CHILDREN

A COUPLE OF STRING TRICKS

HINTS FOR PERFORMERS

ORIGINS AND ACKNOWLEDGEMENTS

THE ACCORDION TO THE DOG

First you need to know how to make the Accordion by heart. Go back to pages 38-49.

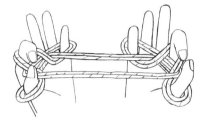

Thumbs touching their own index fingers.

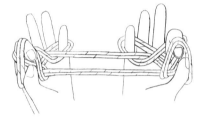

Turn thumb loops onto index fingers.

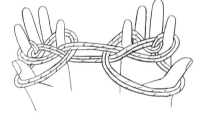

Turn original index loops onto thumbs.

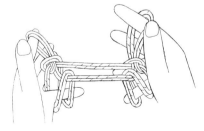

Turn new thumb loops onto little fingers.

The musician has a dog.

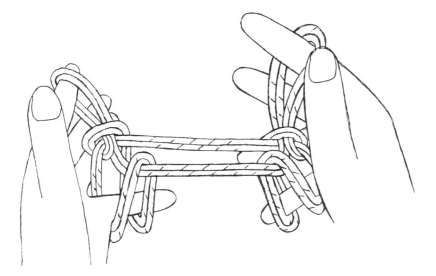

THE DOG

THE DOG TO THE BONE

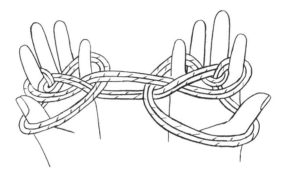

Upper little finger loops return to thumbs.

Release index loops. Pull apart.

It wags its tail because it has

a bone!

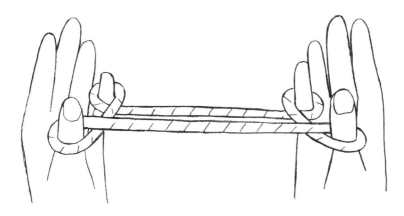

THE BONE

WATER

First you need to DOUBLE THE STRING (see page 52).

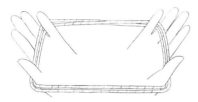

Hold loop in Basic Position on thumbs and little fingers.

Turn only the left palm away. Right hand remains stationary.

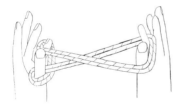

Catch back string on back of thumb and return.

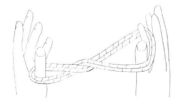

Drop left little finger string.

Left little finger enters left thumb loop from below to widen it (opposite page).
Hands scissor moving central twist to mimic water.

This water is shaking

because...

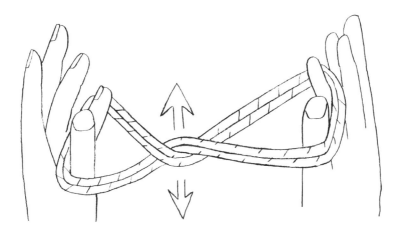

MOVING WATER

WATER TO THE CROCODILE

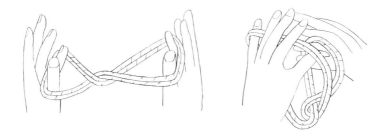

Left thumb places the single left loop first over the stationary right thumb and second over the right little finger

Left thumb continues moving to the left to make the crocodile's tail (opposite page). Pull tail to make the mouth snap.

Note: This is an old crocodile with a knotty tooth and stiff jaw.

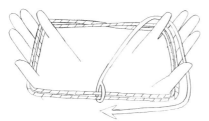

For a young crocodile hold loop in Basic Position

and circle near string once clockwise around right little finger and thumb.

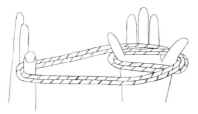

YOUNG CROCODILE

...there is a crocodile in it.

Snap! Snap! Snap!

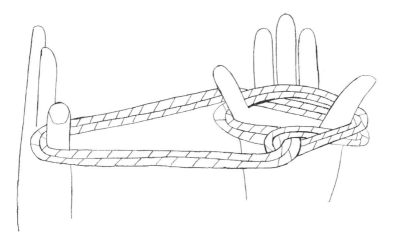

OLD CROCODILE

CUTTING THE HAND

Make Opening 'A' with a single loop. See page 66

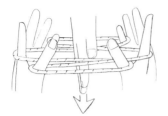

Ask a friend to pass hand through central diamond.

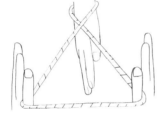

Drop all but thumb strings.

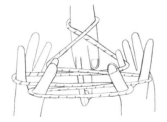

Form Opening 'A' again.

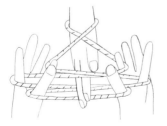

Trapped hand goes *upward* into central diamond.

Drop all but thumb strings again. Hand is released (opposite page).

Are you going to be freed or not? This trick is sometimes called 'Chinese Handcuffs'.

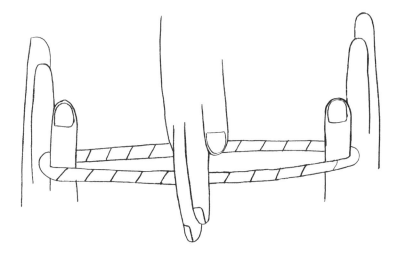

A FREED HAND!

CUTTING THE BODY

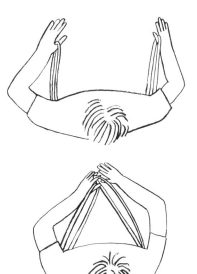

String looping behind back is held by thumbs in front.

Left index enters right thumb loop.

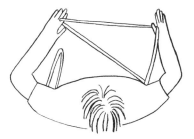

Left index continues to widen right thumb loop as left thumb drops its loop.

Left index and right thumb now hold loop in front! The quicker the better!

Note that these pictures are drawn from above.

The string seems to cut through the body...

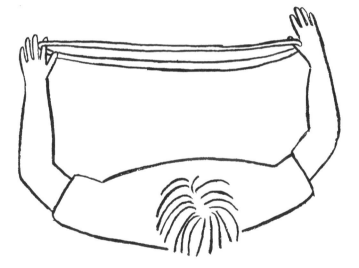

THE KNIFE AND THE SWORD

When you have learnt some string games you can become a Magician, a Story-Teller and a Party-Entertainer all in one!

Performing 'The Birthday Party' is ideal. It repeats itself. If your audience is not quiet the first time round it will be the second! Remember to go slowly so your audience can enjoy every moment. You can show some tricks too and then perhaps teach some figures.

When it comes to teaching, start with something simple, like The Knife. Go slowly, step by step. Remember, even doubling can be difficult to begin with! The quick learners can teach each other and practise variations like The Sword (simply The Knife made with a single loop) while you help the others by moving their fingers.

Now you can become a
Magician, a Story-Teller
and a Party-Entertainer all
in one!

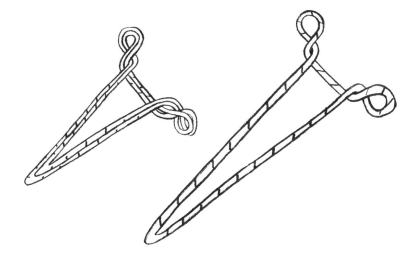

KNIFE   SWORD

MAKING THE TABLE-CLOTH

If you teach the 'Birthday Party' sequence it is simpler to reach the Table-cloth by the following means:

1. Left hand holds up doubled loop.

2. Right hand passes upright, palm away, through loop. 'How!' (fig 1)

3. Right hand returns, except outstretched thumb and little finger which catch sides of loop. (fig 2)

4. Left hand drops loop which swings onto right fore-arm. (fig 3)

5. Left hand claps right fore-arm through loop and returns, all except outstretched thumb and little finger which catch sides of loop. (fig 4)

6. The Table-cloth is ready.

For some, learning as far as the Accordion or Star will be enough. Others will practise again and again until they get the Glasses right! For all who learn something, the string really is a special gift!

This is an easier way to reach the Table-cloth.

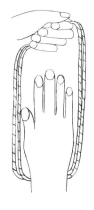

(1)

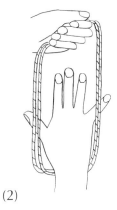

(2)

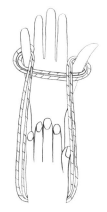

(3)

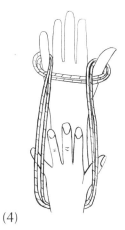

(4)

THE CUP AND SAUCER...

From the Introduction:

The Sunflower, Bell and Racing Car are all original continuations of traditional figures.

The Sea-gull comes from Nunivak Island, Alaska.

The Pig comes from South America.

From 'The Birthday Party':

The Accordion comes from the South Sea Islands where it is known as 'Mrs Crab'.

From the 'Five-pointed Star':

The Star is a result of a task given by Movement Education and Teacher Trainer Jaimen MacMillan to his students, though arrived at by a different means.

Kimberley Nichols, a schoolgirl at Philpots Manor School in Sussex, added the Tuna Sandwich.

My son Raphael learnt the Five-pointed Star on his fifth birthday with a special short string which did not need 'trebling'. He then proceeded to invent the Man and the Wine-glass.

The Cup and Saucer probably comes from New Caledonia, where it is known as the Outrigger Canoe.

NEW CALEDONIA

...AND OTHER FIGURES

A Sharp Knife is an intermediary figure of Caroline Island games.

From 'One day in Paris':

> A version of the words of this well-known sequence was overheard from Sussex children who learnt them from their teacher Martin Baker.

From 'Invented by Children':

> Both the Dog and the Crocodile were 'invented' by Raphael, aged 5.

From 'A Couple of Tricks':

> These tricks are known all over the World.

Cat's Cradle for Two is thought to have been brought to Europe from South East Asia, much like the kite.

THE CRADLE TO THE SAW

Index fingers take long framing strings and lift.

First player keeps middle fingers only.

A last figure: How to make the Saw from the Cradle.

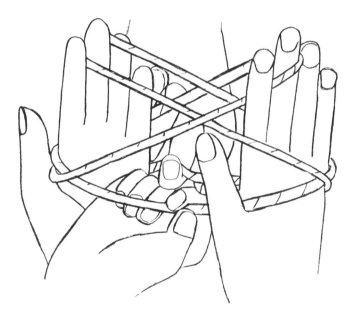

MAKE YOUR OWN LOOP

(With adult supervision)

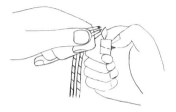

Melt together the slightly frayed ends of a 2 metre length of nylon cord. *Don't get burnt!*

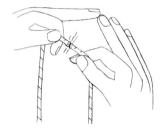

Push ends together. After 5 seconds they hold.

Squeeze and turn rapidly while still hot.

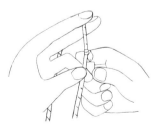

Repeat to smooth join.

Buy nylon cord from a hardware shop and use clothes dye for rainbow colours.

FORTHCOMING BOOK

String Games and Stories Book Two
by Michael Taylor

'Bow and Arrow'. (Shoot an arrow into a tree!)

'Man climbing a tree'. (He climbs one step at a time!)

'The Pig'. (Dancing about in the mud!)

'The Little Bat'. (Opening its wings and flying away.)

'The Racing Car'. (Watch it go!)

More Children's Inventions and Tricks.

Learn how to make The Frog too!

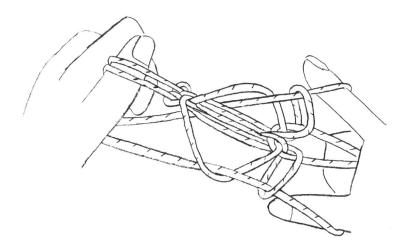

BIBLIOGRAPHY

String Figures and how to make them
by Caroline Furness Jayne.
ISBN 0 486 20152 X.
Dover Books, first published in 1905!

Cat's Cradles and other String Figures
by Joost Elffers & Michael Schuyt.
ISBN 0 14 00 5201 1.
Penguin Books. Unfortunately out of print.

String Games for Beginners
by Kathleen Haddon.
ISBN 85270 049 0. First published in 1934.

Les Ficelles du Conteur
by Anne Pellowski.
ISBN 0 02 044690 X.
This book includes two stories for the cat's cradle
sequence, one by the author and the other by children.

Cat's Cradle and other String Games
Books One and Two
by Camilla Gryski.
ISBN 0 207 15096 and 0 207 15271 3.
These books seem to be out of print.
There are many books by Camilla Gryski available
through the Internet.

About the Author

Michael Taylor is a teacher and movement specialist who promotes traditional childhood skills-games of movement and agility for the classroom, playground and gym which aid co-ordination and are developmental and fun.

His string figure stories have been presented in hospitals, schools, old people's homes and summer camps. One story, 'The Dragon, the Princess and Jack' was specially translated by Claudine, his wife, and shown at the 1st Traditional Games Festival in Berck-sur-mer.

As well as string figures he collects and teaches clapping games, finger games, jump-rope activities, ball bouncing and bean bag games. Some of these will be published in future books.

Michael Taylor has worked in schools with teachers and in hospitals with nurses and play therapists. He gives occasional parties for children – sometimes with his son, Raphael, as his special helper!

More information on INSET (workshops and training) and bulk orders of strings can be obtained from:

Michael Taylor,
9 Kidbrooke Rise
Forest Row
East Sussex
RH18 5LA, UK.

OTHER BOOKS FROM HAWTHORN PRESS

Games Children Play
How Games and Sport Help Children Develop
Kim Brooking-Payne
An accessible guide to games with children of age 3
upwards. These games are all tried and tested, and are the
basis for the author's extensive teacher training work. The
book explores children's personal development and how
this is expressed in movement, play, songs and games.
192 pp; 297 x 210mm; 1 869 890 78 7; paperback.

All Year Round
Ann Druitt, Christine Fynes-Clinton, Marije Rowling
Brimming with things to make; activities, stories, poems and songs to share with your
family. Observing the round of festivals is an enjoyable way to bring rhythm into
children's lives and provide a series of meaningful landmarks to look forward to.
288pp; 250 x 200mm; 1 869 890 47 7; paperback.

The Children's Year
Crafts and Clothes for Children and Parents to make
Stephanie Cooper, Christine Fynes-Clinton, Marije Rowling
Children and parents are encouraged to try all sorts of handwork, with different
projects relating to the seasons of the year.
192pp; 250 x 200mm; 1 869 890 00 0; paperback.

Festivals, Family and Food
Diana Carey and Judy Large
A unique source of stories, recipes, things to make,
activities, poems, songs and festivals.
216pp; 250 x 200mm; 0 950 706 23 X; paperback.

Festivals Together
A Guide to Multicultural Celebration
Sue Fitzjohn, Minda Weston, Judy Large
224pp; 250 x 200mm; 1 869 890 46 9; paperback.

**If you have difficulties ordering *Hawthorn Press* books from a bookshop,
you can order direct from Scottish Book Source Distribution, 137 Dundee
Street, Edinburgh, EH11 1BG. Tel: 0131 229 6800 Fax: 0131 229 9070**

Dear Reader, if you wish to follow up your reading of *Pull the other one!*, please tick any of the boxes below as appropriate, fill in your name and address and return to Michael Taylor.

☐ Please send me details of Michael Taylor's workshops and demonstrations.

☐ Please send me details about ordering strings, including bulk rates.

☐ Please send me details about other books on string games.

Name _____

Address _____

_____

_____ Post code _____

Please return to:
Michael Taylor, 9 Kidbrooke Rise, Forest Row,
East Sussex, RH18 5LA, UK.
Tel: (01342) 824443.